How to Draw
Continuous Lines
For Kids

Author Tony R. Smith

Copyright © 2019 by Tony R. Smith. All Rights Reserved.

No part of this publication may be reproduced, distributed, or transmitted in any form or by any means, including photocopying, recording, or other electronic or mechanical methods, or by any information storage and retrieval system without the prior written permission of Smith Show Publishing, except in the case of very brief quotations embodied in critical reviews and certain other noncommercial uses permitted by copyright law.

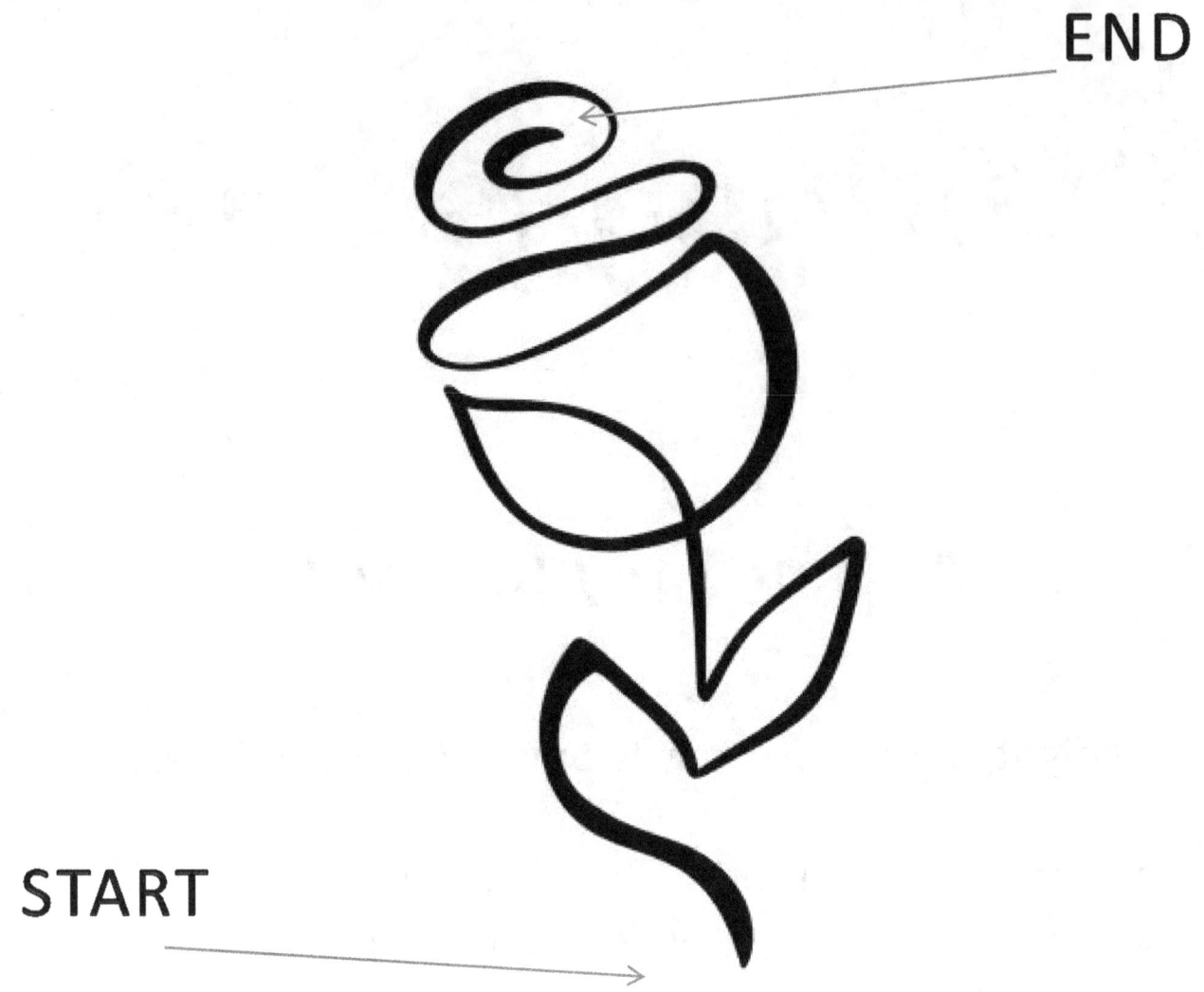

FINAL DRAWING

Continuous line drawing
is a continuous line unbroken
from begging until end.

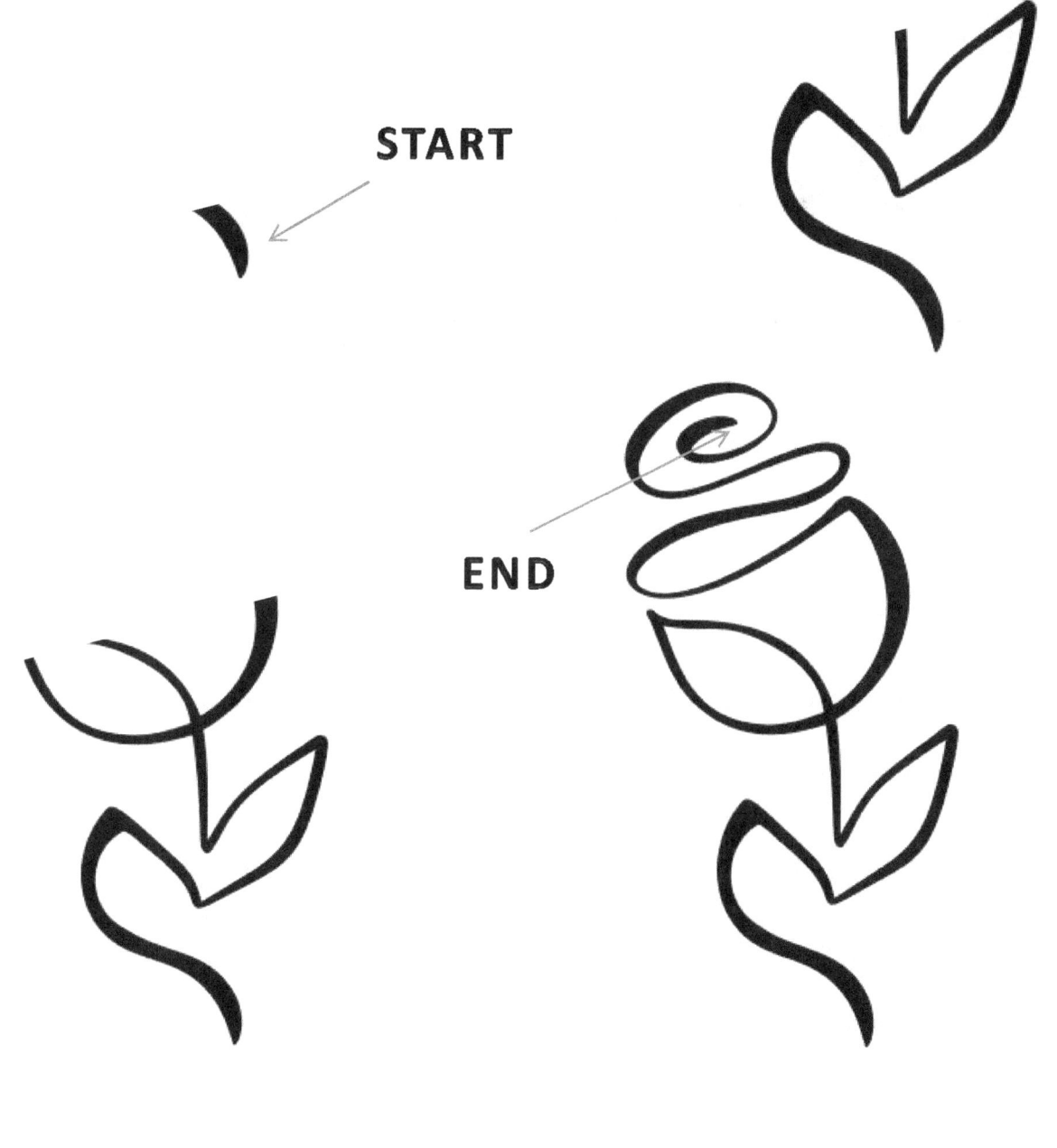

Flower Continuous
Line Drawing

DRAW/SKETCH

DRAW/SKETCH

DRAW/SKETCH

DRAW/SKETCH

DRAW/SKETCH

DRAW/SKETCH

DRAW/SKETCH

DRAW/SKETCH

DRAW/SKETCH

DRAW/SKETCH

DRAW/SKETCH

DRAW/SKETCH

DRAW/SKETCH

Face Continuous Line Drawing

DRAW/SKETCH

DRAW/SKETCH

DRAW/SKETCH

DRAW/SKETCH

DRAW/SKETCH

DRAW/SKETCH

DRAW/SKETCH

DRAW/SKETCH

DRAW/SKETCH

DRAW/SKETCH

DRAW/SKETCH

Animal Continuous Line Drawing

DRAW/SKETCH

DRAW/SKETCH

DRAW/SKETCH

DRAW/SKETCH

DRAW/SKETCH

DRAW/SKETCH

DRAW/SKETCH

DRAW/SKETCH

DRAW/SKETCH

www.ingramcontent.com/pod-product-compliance
Lightning Source LLC
Chambersburg PA
CBHW080023130526
44591CB00036B/2583